SABITA FINDS HER VOICE
BY DR. STEPHANIE VAVILALA
ILLUSTRATED BY JEN A. SHANNON

Copyright © 2021 Therapeutic Expressions, LLC. All Rights Reserved.

No part of this book may be reproduced in any form or by any electronic or mechanical means, including information storage and retrieval systems, without written permission from the author, except in the case of a reviewer, who may quote brief passages embodied in critical articles or in a review. The views and the opinions expressed in this book are those of the author. All content provided is not intended to malign any religion, ethnic group, club, organization, company, or individual.

Distribution by
KDP- Amazon and Ingram Spark
P.O.D.

Printed in the United States of America
Title: Sabita Finds her Voice
Author: Stephanie Vavilala
Illustrator: Jen A. Shannon
Editor: Brooke Vitale
Publicity: Talk+Tell

ISBNs
Hardcover: 978-1-7367083-0-9
Paperback: 978-1-7367083-1-6
EBook: 978-1-7367083-2-3

Publisher: Therapeutic Expressions, LLC.

Book description: Follow Sabita, a brave young girl who has autism and is non-verbal as she goes on an adventure to find a special way to communicate her hopes and dreams.

DEDICATION

Dearest Sabita,

You inspired me before you were ever born and are a God given gift to me! Throughout my infertility journey, you were preparing me to be able to overcome difficult challenges and never give up. You showed me the best things in life were the things worth working hard for. You taught me a different way to communicate and helped me to embrace how words can be spoken through the use of technology.

Your "words" are louder and stronger than anyone I know. You have inspired me to speak these words to the world on your behalf. Your words will, no doubt, continue to have a positive impact in the world! I know, through this book, you will inspire many other children to find their voice.

XOXO,

Mom

Sabita was like other girls her age.
She had hopes. She had dreams.

Although Sabita could make sounds, she could not make words. And that made Sabita sad.

THIRSTY
SAD
HUGS
FRIEND
HAPPY
COLD
DOG
BEACH
MOMMY
DADDY
HUNGRY
PLAY
HOME

She wanted to share her thoughts, but she could not. They were locked deep inside her.

Sabita could express herself a little by drawing pictures, but it was not enough.

More than anything in the world, Sabita wanted to have a voice!

So, her Mommy set out to find one.

After months and months of searching, Sabita's mommy found what she was looking for.

Opening their tablet, she showed Sabita the new App she'd bought.

Sabita touched a picture, and the App said the word out loud! She touched a word, and the App said it!

Sabita was so happy.
Finally, she had a way to communicate!

With her new voice Sabita could ask her daddy to do one of her favorite things.

With her new voice Sabita could ask for one of her favorite things to eat.

With her new voice Sabita could

talk to her friends and teacher at school.

With her new voice Sabita could play games with her friends.

With her new voice Sabita could say how excited she was to go on vacation and ride in an airplane.

With her new voice Sabita could tell her doctor when she wasn't feeling well.

With her new voice Sabita could talk to her dogs.

With her new voice Sabita could say, "I love you."

With her new voice, Sabita could answer people when they asked why she couldn't speak.

I CAN! THIS IS MY VOICE! AND JUST LOOK HOW MUCH I HAVE TO SAY!

Author's Note

Writing 'Sabita Finds Her Voice' was more than just a labor of love. It's the life that I, as well as many others around the globe, find themselves living day in and day out.

My husband, Raj, and I struggled with infertility, so when we found out we were pregnant with Sabita, we were over the moon. It wasn't until she was around 18 months old that we began to notice she was, well, different. Having worked as a therapist in mental health, I knew we needed to have her evaluated for autism.

Once Sabita was diagnosed, I began to immerse myself in everything I could regarding autism, including going back to school to become a Board Certified Behavior Analyst. I wanted to help her any way I could.

As she grew older and was not speaking, we had to come up with some type of communication for her. I watched Sabita in her frustrations with not being able to communicate verbally and I knew I had to find something. Her words were there, but she couldn't speak them. The app I found on her iPad has made an incredible world of difference in her life and being able to communicate in a world that communicates verbally.

I sincerely hope you find 'Sabita Finds Her Voice' inspiring, even if your child does not have autism or isn't non-verbal. This book can help educate your child about a different type of communication and how to embrace other children who may have autism and/or be non-verbal. For more information, visit SabitaSpeaks.org. There, you can learn more about how you can help provide this much needed technology for other non-verbal children.

I want to take the time to thank my husband, Raj, for his love and support through this entire journey. Your encouragement behind my ideas is irreplaceable. I would like to thank my mom, who always encouraged me speak my truth and modeled how to use words for the betterment of the world. Thanks to my sisters, who always listened to what I had to say and supported my journey to speak them to the world. Many thanks to my friends who have been nothing but supportive in all my efforts. Lastly, thanks to Jen Shannon who brought my book to life with her amazing illustrations.

Illustrator's Note

Stephanie and I met 6 years ago when she was referred to me for head shots by a local photographer. I was a portrait photographer with a studio location in St. Augustine and specialized in women's portraits.

I've photographed Stephanie and Sabita quite a bit throughout the years and have watched Stephanie not only dream big, but bring those dreams to fruition. She's an amazing woman with a heart of gold. This book is an amazing labor of love. I'm so blessed to be a part of telling part of Sabita's journey.

Having always been an artist, I've learned many art forms over my lifetime, including illustration. When Stephanie asked me to illustrate her debut children's book, it was a big yes!

Having never illustrated a children's book, I learned so much about the process. Many times, as an artist, you have a tendency to keep taking things further and to be as detailed as possible. This process taught me how to think like a child (which you'd think I'd be good at since I have four of my own!), keep things simple and not overcomplicate ideas. After Sabita's character came to life, the rest flowed freely into this beautiful story about Sabita and her ability to communicate in a world centered around verbal communication.

My favorite spread in this book is Sabita eating her chips. There's something about watching a child eat something they REALLY enjoy that makes me laugh and fills me with joy. It's a childlike playfulness; like a mischevious smirk that says, "Oooo! This is REALLY good! Am I actually allowed to eat this?" or a silly dance in the kitchen. That's what I wanted to portray in this spread.

My hope is that these illustrations will help others to connect emotionally with the feelings associated with overcoming frustrations to feeling freedom; like they can do anything they set their mind to do. This book will not only help kids learn to interact with children with autism that are also non-verbal, but will help others to know that there are resources out there to assist in helping their child communicate.

Lasty, thank you, Stephanie, for trusting me to bring your vision to life. You're amazing! Shine on! XOXO.

CPSIA information can be obtained
at www.ICGtesting.com
Printed in the USA
BVHW061205290421
606128BV00002B/150